Champion! Your W
Powerful Motivational
Your Suc

Aiming to Heal

Copyright 2023
Chistell Publishing
https://www.chistell.com
First Printing, August 2023

All rights reserved

Published by: Chistell Publishing
                7235 Aventine Way, Suite #201
                Chattanooga, TN 37421

Author: Denise Turney
ISBN: 979-8-9856651-4-7

Dedication

For my son.

I love you, Gregory –

Table of Contents

Chapter 1 – What You Really Want

    Get Clear About What You Really Want

    Listen to Your True Self

    Certainty Matters

Chapter 2 – Start with Power

    Believe

    Clarify Smart Actions

    Take Action

Chapter 3 – Goal Vision Anchor

    Focus

    Let The Vision Lead You

    Stay Anchored

Chapter 4 – Navigating the Middle

    About the Middle

    Middle Ground Challenges

    Advancing Beyond the Middle

Chapter 5 – Keep Advancing

    Live "Quit" Free

    Be Unstoppable

    Persist

Chapter 6 – Unstuck

    Working Through Stoppages

    Emotional Struggles

    You Can Do It

Chapter 7 – SOAR

    Keep Climbing

    Meeting Success

    Celebrate Every Win

Chapter 8 – Life Wide Open

    Design a Beautiful Life

    Fun! Fun! Fun!

    Loving What You Do

Chapter 9 – Make It an Adventure

    Revisit Excitement

    New Things Ahead

    Look Around

Chapter 10 – Rewarding Relationships

    Rich Connections

    Make Them Good

    Let Them Know

Chapter 11 – What's Next

    Let the Next Vision Surface

    Stay Open

    Your Work Is Needed

    You Are Love – You Are Loved

Get Ready 2 Unleash Your Inner Champion

About – Champion! Your Will to Win is Key! Powerful Motivational Quotes to Support Your Success

It's exciting to receive a big dream! Yet, the path to fulfilling a big dream isn't smooth or simple. Short motivational messages can keep you on track. Motivational messages bolster momentum as you work toward fulfilling a big dream or a big goal, creating rewarding patterns and designing a beautiful life. That is what this book aims to do.

Naturally, motivation is a fuel, providing ample energy to keep advancing. Yet, benefits aside, it's not always easy to approach life with motivation.

If you've ever had an idea surface in your consciousness, felt exhilaration, wonder and hope, only to shift into frustration, agitation and confusion a day later – because someone told you the idea was preposterous, a pipe dream or impossible to fulfill - you know why motivation is so important. Add in your busy schedule, relationships to manage, work and finances, and you can see how quickly a strong inspiration can be ripped from you.

This is where your will to win matters. Your will to win takes you beyond poking at and nurturing a goal or a dream. The will to win propels you to research and study a goal, identifying resources you'll need to manifest the goal.

Stay motivated and, before you know it, you'll start taking smart actions – the very actions that shift you from where you are now to where you want to be. As this happens more, your journey sweetens.

This book is designed with chapters that focus on key success areas. Reading Champion! Your Will to Win is Key! Powerful Motivational Quotes to Support Your Success puts you in touch with motivational quotes, empowering messages you can read within seconds.

Consider reading at least one quote from the book daily. It is a choice that could shield you from negative feedback you might receive about your work, creative arts, dreams or even your destiny.

Beyond that, stay open to being inspired to take smart actions. Allow your true Self to guide you into more and more good. Here's to hoping that this book, Champion! Your Will to Win is Key! Powerful Motivational Quotes to Support Your Success, becomes a rewarding resource on your amazing journey.

Chapter 1 – What Do You Really Want

Desire is the foundation of every dream. Sounds exhilarating until you consider how many times a day you want something.

If your mind isn't busy coming up with desires, you read or hear something that sparks a longing in you. For instance, let a friend tell you about the fun she had visiting another country, hoteling in a cabin by the river, and the desire to travel might spring up within you.

You see a suit, hairstyle or art piece that you think is attractive and – what do you feel? Desire.

In a single day, you could experience this half a dozen times, about six different things. Getting clear about what you *really* want is a must. Otherwise, you could feel like a ping pong ball, bouncing from one dream or goal to another – not one of the goals fulfilled.

Get Clear About What You Really Want

Clarity is a mental light. The clearer you get about your goal, the easier it can become to not only see where you are now, but the simpler it can be to transition from where you *really* are to where you *really* want to be.

The next motivational quotes focus on clarity. Empower yourself with the spirit in these messages, fueling your biggest dreams. While you read these quotes, pause and consider what you truly want, breaking the desire into parts, even asking yourself **why** you want what you say you do.

Clarity is your natural state

Lighting the way

Always where you are

Eager to reveal itself

The instant you're ready to accept

what you already know

Dig, probe, get curious

Until the path clears

Opening up the way you should go

Remember when your mind was clear?

You knew just what to do

Who to connect with

How to move forward

That clarity remains – inside your mind

Tap into It

Meditate if you must

Sit still

Get to know your true Self

This Self knows what you should do NOW

Big dreams plus clarity

Equals approaching success

"However long the night,

The dawn will break."

African Proverb

Within you is a light

Follow the light

Listen to Your True Self

In stillness and in quiet-mind-ness, you can hear your true Self, communicating with you, sharing its love with you. Gone is the seeming need to listen to another person tell you what your true Self is communicating; you'll hear clearly for yourself.

This Self is what you really are. It knows the way. Whether you're dealing with relationships, work, leisure, creative arts, financial, spiritual, emotional or physical change, there is a part of you that knows today's step.

Cultivate the art of listening to your true Self. Make this a daily practice and you will start to connect with truth that's communicating with you. Today, you might refer to this as "picking up a vibe" or "knowing something that's rooted in love that you can't explain."

Beyond this world

Is a place

Deep within you

Where clarity, knowledge and wisdom are. You can access this place and

Live a marvelous life

"I can do all things through Christ who gives me strength."

Philippians 4:13

"Don't fear an ill wind if your haystacks are tied down – There is no need to worry about things if you're properly prepared."

Irish Proverb

Breath by breath

Step by step

Follow your Higher Self

It's creating a journey of wonder and awe

How beautiful is the vision that your true Self holds of you.

Miracles and success are natural.

Keep advancing – you'll see how true this is.

Certainty Matters

Once you gain clarity about your big dream and strengthen the dream by quieting your mind, allowing your true Self to be heard from within, you enter a state of certainty. It's this certainty that causes you to know what you really want.

Should you hit snags or challenges, certainty will cause you to see that what you're going through is worth it. After all, you're not progressing toward hardship. Instead, you're progressing toward a magnificent goal.

Moving toward a goal with certainty puts you on solid ground. Talk about being steady on your feet as you advance.

In certainty and sureness is a good foundation

Be still until you gain certainty about what it is you should do

"If you forsake a certainty for an uncertainty, you will lose both the certainty and the uncertainty."

Sanskrit Proverb

Being certain about what you *really* want to do is as important as knowing how to do what you want to do.

Chapter 2 – Start with Power

You could change your life. Within seconds, you could be headed toward new experiences, relationships and career and spiritual adventures.

Depending on how you start, the change could be exciting, filling you with hope. Or you could enter a period of uncertainty, not what you want. Therefore, start strong. Start with power.

If you've seen a sprinter burst out of blocks, leaping several yards into the heart of a championship race, you know the value of a powerful start. The following writings and motivational quotes help you zone in on starting with power as you move toward your goals.

Believe

Believe in yourself as a creation of Source. Believe in the love-based endeavor you want to fulfill. Believe from the start.

This is important, because when you believe in your true Self, you gain the confidence to get started. But not only will you get started, you'll start with power.

Seeking inspiration? Look no further. Read on and see if you don't come away feeling stronger, equipped with the confidence and the trust to believe in your dreams.

"As you go the way of life you will see a great chasm. Jump. It is not as wide as you think."

Native American Proverb

The first step is the most important step, because without taking it, all other steps are impossible.

If fear can't stop you from believing enough to get started, it can't stop you at all.

You'll never know how much you can do if you never get started.

Success has a funny way of linking the end to the beginning.

Clarify Smart Actions

Clarify smart actions you will take to achieve your goals. To help with this, consider writing down specific steps (include due dates) that you will take to get from where you are now to where you want to be. Get very specific when mapping out these steps. Also, identify resources you'll need.

Spreadsheets, journals, ledgers and project planning templates are great tools to use to map out clarifying actions. Take your time identifying and writing down actions that will take you step-by-step to your goals.

Within you is the ability to focus, bringing the right actions into view.

Like an engine revving, signaling that a car is ready to power forward, clarity can charge your dreams with an unstoppable power.

You can't see the finish from where you are, but if you start now, you can see the next step.

Take Action

Now that you've clarified what you really want and have outlined the specific steps that you will take to achieve your goal, it's time to start taking those smart actions.

The sooner you get started - now that you've identified resources, steps to take and are certain that you should pursue your dream – the better.

Putting 15 minutes into your dream right now is better than waiting until tomorrow to get started. It could be as simple as making a telephone call, sending an email or drafting a letter. Just start taking smart action.

Nothing changes until you choose wisely and take action.

All great achievements have a beginning.

"God helps those who help themselves."

Australian Proverb

Life in this dream-world is a long journey only made worthwhile by taking one courageous love-based action after another.

You'll never prove to yourself how much you believe in you if you don't take your first smart action.

Chapter 3 – Goal Vision Anchor

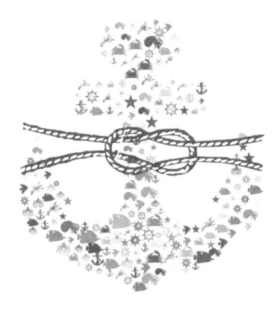

Just as it sounds, a goal vision anchor keeps you from drifting, floating away from what you set out to experience. In a busy world that's filled with information, deadlines and distractions, an anchor is essential.

For you, an anchor might be a mantra that's linked to your core values. Or it might be an image that elicits strong emotion and faith. A scripture, poem, song or an incredibly powerful saying could also serve as an anchor.

To be effective, an anchor must hold. Not only do you need to believe in it, an anchor must hold up regardless of how you feel, regardless of what you're going through.

Focus

Make a commitment to stay focused on your dream. At first glance, staying focused on your dream might not appear critical. However, the further you progress, the more new experiences, new people and new places you'll meet.

It's easy to get distracted by the newness. If you're not alert, you could start moving toward a different goal than what you had set out to obtain. So, stay focused and committed to your dream.

Feeling discouraged because you've experienced a setback? Refocus on your dream; refocus on your goal. Is life feeling too hard, like you're facing one bad thing after another?

Focus on your dream. Set your attention on your goal.

Be limber, flexible, open – moving with the eye of a tiger. Sharpen your focus as the time spent pursuing your goal extends.

Focusing reduces stress because it makes it easier for your brain to zone in on what's important.

Focus to sharpen your aim and produce higher quality work.

Let the Vision Lead You

See yourself stepping into your dream. See yourself doing what you most want to do. What are you wearing? Where are you living? Who are the people you're with? What are you doing to relax? Where do you go when you want to have fun? What are you eating? Where do you go for exercise? How do you spend your time working? What are you doing as it regards stilling your mind and connecting with the Creator?

Get specific. Actually see yourself doing what you love.

Do colors in the location show in your mind when you visualize what you're doing? Are there any scents?

Hold this vision. Use your imagination to keep this vision at the front of your mind's eye. As you focus on this vision, it becomes a magnet, pulling you, leading you.

Let the light you need to see – light embedded in the inner eye, creating vision – show you the way.

Follow the inner light. It's eager to lead you down glorious pathways you haven't thought about or heard of.

We know how to proceed when we still our mind and access the light that is within us.

Stay Anchored

Hold the vision to stay anchored. Stay free of letting outcomes determine whether your dream is worth continuing to pursue. Not every outcome will be what you want. There will be setbacks as well as great forward strides.

Recall the instant you were first visited by your dream. How did the dream introduce itself to you? Was it in a nightdream, a vision (an actual inner vision), through something you read, etc.?

Meditate on the root of your dream, including how the dream first came to you. Think about the benefits to you and others that will be harvested after your dream is fulfilled. Stay anchored.

"A tree cannot stand without roots."

Congolese Proverb

Tough times test the strength of your dream's anchor.

In order to succeed, we need a dependable anchor, a foundational core that will not give way under pressure.

Success does not happen simply because you want it to. You need clear vision, perseverance, flexibility, passion and a strong anchor.

Chapter 4 – Navigating the Middle

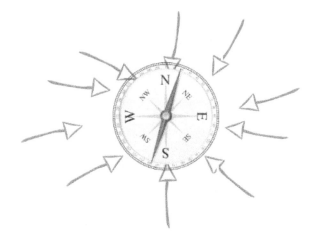

If one area feels more intimating than the start of a dream, it's the middle. Huge congratulations to you on getting started with power and for continuing to move forward. Should desired occurrences seem to have slowed, you could be in the middle.

Events move slowly in the middle. Impatience can become a challenge in the middle. And it makes sense. You've been working to fulfill your dream for months, perhaps years. To say you're ready for the dream to fully manifest may be a huge understatement.

Hold to your dream. Sharpen your vision if necessary. If you don't quit (and you won't), you'll move through this stage and get that much closer to the full manifestation of your dream!

About the Middle

Because you might spend months or years in the middle, you could experience restlessness, impatience, frustration, isolation and aloneness. That's right. You might feel as if you're the only one going through what you are.

A period of transformation, being in evolution and rebirth are words and terms used to describe the middle. What you won't be short on while you're in the middle is discomfort.

You've heard it said that great transformation and tremendous success does not come during moments of comfort. Well. Your great time has arrived if you're in the middle.

The following motivational quotes focus on the middle, aim to help you get through this challenging phase in full strength, with hope and resilience.

"We will be known forever by the tracks we leave."

First Nations Proverb

Don't rush the process.

Though it can be hard and long, life's greatest treasures are often birthed while in the middle.

Push when you feel squeezed.

The juice of life is in the middle.

Greatness bursts forth if you push.

Middle Ground Challenges

In addition to feeling uncertain, uncomfortable and isolated, while in middle ground, you might actually feel physically off balance. Back and neck pain and stiffness or joint soreness are other physical symptoms that could signal you're in middle ground.

Worse than these symptoms, you might feel that, regardless of what you do or how hard and long you work, nothing changes. Of all middle ground challenges, this is the most painful.

Re-read the opening chapters of this book. Focus on what's shared, the importance of getting clear about what you really want, identifying and clarifying smart actions you'll take to achieve your goals. Above all, recall why you got started and recommit to finishing. The middle will release you and you will take forward leaps.

What is seen in light remains, is never forgotten, never forsaken, not even while one is in the middle.

Keeping your focus fixed on the goal can make you flow through the middle, moving that much closer to the finish.

Leave nothing behind as you exit the middle. Bring every lesson along on the remaining parts of your journey.

Advancing Beyond the Middle

Believe it or not, middle ground is a place of great inner transformation. Once you reach middle ground, even if you go back to the start (move back to an old house, return to an old relationship, revisit a former habit), you will never be the same.

Path through middle ground challenges is to keep advancing.

Are you tempted to quit your dream? Think about how uncomfortable it feels in the middle. Do you want to stay in this place? Remember the other option is to go back which leads to boredom, fatigue and flatness.

Also, know that after you move through the middle, you're closer to goal fulfillment. Goal fulfilled, you could become a life teacher, showing others how to get through the middle and manifest their biggest dreams.

"Even in the middle of the night, God is kind."

Afghanistan Proverb

"There isn't a flood which will not subside."

Scottish Proverb

You'll know when you leave the middle phase. Joy will come to you like a welcomed release. Courage you used to navigate the middle will serve you twice as much now.

Let me go, middle, in your wise timing. I will continue. I will reach my goal, fulfilling my destiny.

Chapter 5 – Keep Advancing

Advancing is defined as moving forward with purpose. Developing or creating a service, product, resource or artform is also defined as advancing.

Clearly, you're in process when you're advancing. As a writer the actual process of writing is a form of advancing. Each stroke a painter colors a blank canvas with is a form of advancing.

Every step a dancer takes, stepping, tapping, spinning and turning on the floor, is a form of advancing. Seen this way, it's clear that each single action you take is critical as it regards fullness, the completion of what you are doing.

If headwinds feel too strong, pause but don't quit. Another effective choice is to focus on the current step and only this step. Simply focus on the step you're taking right now.

Live Quit Free

Quitting may feel good, offering a sense of relief. But this relief only lasts for so long. Why? The dream inside you is still there. It doesn't go away just because you quit.

No matter what you do after you quit, you might have a nagging feeling that something is missing. You know that feeling you get when you step outside your door and immediately you start feeling like you left something important in the house.

As it regards your dream, forget trying to use your conscious mind to rid of the feeling. It's coming from deeper inside you. Even if it seems to vanish, it will pop back into the center of your thought system.

In other words, even if you quit, a deeper part of you never will. Avoid feeling split and be honest with yourself. Don't quit. Instead, go get what you truly want.

Quitting turns your best experiences into no more than these four words: "what might have been"

Quitting what you know you should finish is telling yourself that you don't trust YOU enough to believe YOU can do what it takes to achieve your goals.

Leap - if you feel like quitting on what you know you should do.

Jump right over the "quit" barrier. You can do it. Nothing can stop you.

Be Unstoppable

Once you become unstoppable, you can see how powerful your mind is. Commit to being unstoppable, and you'll see how your mind comes up with ideas, some remarkably creative, to get around internal and external obstacles.

The observer in you can witness how flexible and dependable your mind is. Hence, your commitment to being unstoppable teaches you a lot about yourself.

This, in turn, builds your confidence to try new things. Be unstoppable and you watch your mind find a way through the most challenging, most painful and hardest experiences.

You might even shock yourself.

Be unstoppable because it's the way to gain more than a goal fulfilled. It's a way to learn more about yourself.

You're unstoppable. That's what you are. Obstacles move aside as you approach. Every hindrance knows you are a champion because you refuse to stop, fueled by vision and a most worthwhile goal.

Prove to yourself what you're created with. Be unstoppable!

The deepest sense of victory comes after you surmount the desire to quit, keep climbing, and reach a pinnacle.

Persist

To persist means more than not quitting. You need something to keep striving for when you persist. You don't keep going for the sake of not quitting.

There's a goal, a target, that you set and keep your sights on. Regardless of what happens, you focus your energies to hit this target.

Persist and you'll learn to distinguish between what's important (what moves you toward goal fulfillment) and what is a distraction. You might find it surprising how many conversations, news stories, people and events pop up during your journey – simply to distract you.

Persist to brush away distractions. Persist and your path will become clearer.

Persist. Persist. Persist.
You're victorious and persist is what the victorious do.

Persist so you can look back and admire the view. Persist so you can live in awe of what lies around and ahead.

"Be not afraid of growing slowly, only of staying still."

Chinese Proverb

Persistence is the genesis of greatness.

Chapter 6 – Unstuck

These chapters focus on keys that work together, that often must work together, as if they were good friends, to get you from where you are now to where you want to be. Persistence is required to work yourself free should you get stuck.

To free yourself from being stuck, you may need to still your mind. Safe walks through nature, meditating and simply sitting in silence may prove effective.

As silly as it might sound, changing your diet could also work. For instance, if yours is a diet heavy with greasy foods, carbohydrates and red meat, you might shift out of being stuck if you add more fresh water, fresh fruit and vegetables to your diet.

Yoga, running long distances, swimming and sitting near water could also help you become unstuck. These relaxing activities can pry your thoughts away from what's troubling you, working you toward freedom.

Working Through Stoppages

The best way to deal with stoppages as you work to manifest your goal is to *avoid* blockages. It is true. An ounce of prevention is worth more than a pound of cure.

Whether you aim to avoid stoppages or have already been stopped and need to get going again, consider these easy practices. To begin, add three things that you love to your day.

For example, you could enjoy a daily bubble bath, a bike ride and you could listen to your favorite music at least once a day. Once a week, do a fourth activity that you love, something that excites you.

Shake up your routines. For instance, you could drive through a new part of the region you live in. Or you could spend a night in a tiny house. Changes to your routines help keep you from falling into ruts, help keep you from getting stuck.

Alter course, try a new strategy, ask hard questions, seek advice from those who are where you are trying to be. Stay open. Rest. Start again, but do not stop pursuing a worthwhile goal.

"It's easier to give birth than to think about it."

Japanese Proverb

Ask water. It knows how to yield, flow - work through stoppages.

Look at what's trying to stop you. Examine it, but don't give into it. Find a way and keep going.

Emotional Struggles

Charting a course that leads you closer to your goal is no small fete. It's likely going to require great effort. The great effort that you put in will create emotional surges within you.

In fact, you might feel levels of excitement, hope, fear, happiness, peace, frustration and anticipation that you have not experienced before. These high emotional levels could push you into a daydreaming state, at times.

At other times, high emotional levels could pummel you to downward depths you don't want to enter. You could drop low enough emotionally to convince yourself that the best thing you could ever do is to quit.

Fortunately, there are ways to handle emotional struggles. Journaling, speaking with a friend, effective therapy, reading books about others who have successfully managed emotional struggles and watching documentaries that show a person coming out victorious over emotional struggles can help you navigate this rocky terrain.

Emotions are effective guides, showing you when you're on track or off course. Yet, you must not let emotions bully or push you around. You must keep the keys, especially when emotions rock and charge.

Command emotions with thoughts, steering them as you go along the way.

Water dreams with tears from struggles. Let success sun over all you've come through.

You Can Do It

You can do it! You can do it! Keep telling yourself that. Yet don't just repeat the words, take smart actions, the very actions that lead you, step-by-step, to your destination.

Feeling positive, motivated and encouraged right now? The words "You can do it!" likely feel believable and empowering.

Feeling doubtful, worried and anxious? The words may feel like an annoyance, too hard to believe.

It's for this reason that you need to find one or more ways to remind yourself that you can, indeed, do it! You can fulfill your destiny.

A positive morning routine where you read three empowering quotes or scripture are effective. You could also meditate on a personal mantra you created - a mantra that elicits great emotion from within you.

Look at how much you have accomplished. Look at how much you have hurdled, scaled. Look and you'll see when it comes to manifesting your goals – this too – you can do!

Achievement

Puts what you can do on Full Display

WHEN BIG DREAMS COME TRUE
You may open more to
Your one true Self

"If ye have faith as a grain of mustard seed, ye shall say unto this mountain, remove hence to yonder place, and it shall remove; and nothing shall be impossible unto you."

Matthew 17:20 (KJV)

Chapter 7 – SOAR

It's time to celebrate! You got started, taking smart actions, toward the fulfillment of your big dreams, of your goals. Even more, you've moved through distractions, emotional struggles and the formidable "middle".

You should feel tremendously good about what you have done! Spread your arms like an eagle spreading its wings. It's time to soar!

This is no time to play it small. This is no time to try to hide or diminish what you have done. Soar, amazing YOU! Soar!

As you do, enjoy reading motivational quotes on the following pages that celebrate how far you have come. The view only gets better from here as you continue.

Keep Climbing

By now, you've discovered that you are eternal. For you, there is no end. Your one true Self rest in joy and peace. The journey that you undertook has shown you a little of what you're created with.

You've learned that you are stronger than you thought you were. Working with inner vision, clarity and the light within has hopefully taught you that you are not a body.

Instead, you are projecting part of yourself into a body. Because there is so much more to learn as you continue to awaken to truth, you must keep climbing.

You're headed toward your center. When you get there, you'll appreciate everything that happened along the way.

Climbing strengthens your core.

Climbing is walking in the best direction – UP – which is also WITHIN!

Keep climbing!

You know you can go higher and higher.

Meeting Success

Hello, "You!" Meet success! You've been progressing toward this friend since you began. Success has been waiting to meet and connect with you, patient but eager like a gentle pal.

Take your time getting to know each other. Just as you did when you met other people on your path, you're going to feel different. Emotions may feel light, fun, inviting.

You're no longer afraid to be acknowledged for the good that you do. The days when you blushed because someone complimented you or commented on how much ground you've covered are in the past.

Success is what you do. You are successful and you handle success with gentleness, with love. But that's what friends do.

Enjoy the success you've gained. You earned it. Remember you are more than what you achieve. True success is loving what you do and loving your true Self.

Success is what you do.

Success has been waiting for you to accept it since you started on this path.

Celebrate Every Win

Celebrate every win. Why? There's more ahead. Remember. You're eternal. Taking the time to celebrate every win is your way of confirming that you go on and on, free of an end.

Celebrate every win because you should be compensated for the emotional struggles, distractions and challenges you encountered. You'll remember these small celebrations when you start your next journey.

They will serve as powerful reminders of what you can do. They will strengthen you for what's ahead, motivating, inspiring and encouraging you.

Forget playing it small. Be your loudest, most passionate cheerleader – whether you're winning or learning something new.

Until you celebrate your successes no other celebration you're given will have lasting impact.

Celebrations are milestones that should not be ignored.

All the cheering in the world won't matter until you start rooting for you

Chapter 8 - Life Wide Open

Living life wide open births joy, excitement, peace, anticipation and a rewarding hope. Gone are the repetitive days, instances when you think the same thoughts that you thought the day before and the day before and the day before and . . .

Now that you're living life wide open, you're exploring new thoughts. New ideas are popping into your consciousness.

Because your thoughts are changing, emotions you're dealing with are changing too. You're happier, more hopeful and willing to accept responsibility for your life.

Get out and explore the earth. Travel. Meet new people. Examine your perceptions, being open to seeing an old belief, situation or relationship a new way, in more love and light.

Say good-bye to comfort and hello to newness!

Design a Beautiful Life

You may have been running from this truth. It's not your mother's life. It's not your father's life. It's not your spouse's life. It's not your child's or your friend's life.

This is your life.

It's time to see the connection between your thoughts and your experiences. For instance, if you wake each morning with a groan and tell yourself the day is already ruined (I did this for years), do you find your relationships improving, work you do more rewarding or your energy lifting?

Or do these and other areas of your life suffer, as if falling in step with your thoughts? This may be hard to accept, even harder to change, because it takes focus, awareness, honesty and energy to cease thinking errors and start renewing your mind.

Yet, it's worth it because there is no other way to design a beautiful life.

Choose thoughts wisely.

They are designing the life you live.

Beauty is in the eye of the beholder.

Look back and assess what you see.

How beautiful is the life you've made?

(*Be sure to zone in on the good parts*)

You can change it! You can change it!

Go a new way, turn, leap - do something new!

Fun! Fun! Fun!

There's a lot to be said for a diet. As some share, you are what you eat and drink. But what about your thought diet? Do you pay attention to the thoughts you focus on? Do you think your thoughts impact *how* you perceive, experience life and how you feel?

Considering your life's diet, how much fun do you ensure you take in each day? Remember a carefree time in your life, even if it lasted only for a day? Remember when you looked at your life as a living experience filled with enthusiasm and vigor?

You couldn't wait to see what would come! Whatever it was, you knew you were ready!

Get back to that way of living! Fill each day with fun!

Choose what births joy in you!

Your life is going to fill up regardless of what you do. Why not fill your life with activities you find fun!

"Joy is in the voice of love."

Hawaiian Proverb

A day without fun is a day not well lived

Loving What You Do

If you've poured yourself into a dream, you know how important it is to love what you do. Hours, days, sometimes years, are spent rehashing ideas, building foundational frameworks and creating products and services you're passionate about sharing with others.

Regardless of how successful you are at what you do, technology, social and cultural shifts demand that you change how you create and share what you love. Shifts, losses, stumbles, wins – it's all part of the process.

Which is why it's crucial that you love what you do. Doing what you love allows the joy that you experience - simply by doing what you love - to be your greatest payout. Do what you love and your internal payout is limitless.

Joy is a salary impossible to beat. It's granted to those who do what they love.

Doing what you love shortens the path to creating a life that overflows with peace and joy.

All the success in the world won't mean anything if you don't love what you do.

Chapter 9 – Make It an Adventure

Adventure is impossible inside a life of routine. Life's boring when you think, do and feel the same thing day after day.

You have to let your life be shaken up to explore and enjoy experiencing life as an adventure. Looking for ideas? Call a friend you haven't spoken with in over 10 years. Ride a bike for the first time as an adult. Sing and dance on your back porch the next time it rains.

Striving to make life an adventure may help you to welcome detours and changes you encounter with a sense of wonder instead of dread. Another blessing associated with adventure is that it can remind you that you're only here for a while.

Experience pain – it won't last. Experience success here – it's temporary.

So, get going! A world of adventure awaits!

Revisit Excitement

Set intervals when you'll revisit how you felt when the dream or the goal you're now pursuing first came to you. It could be on a Friday evening or Saturday afternoon when you sit down and recall how thrilled you felt, how you bubbled with enthusiasm and anticipation, the instant you knew what you truly wanted to do in this world.

Don't wait until you face a setback or until you feel discouraged. Similar to how you schedule vacation, schedule time to revisit the exuberance you felt when your dream was brand new.

Earlier you got clear about your goals and the smart actions you'll take to fulfill your goals. Now, *simply let yourself get excited about your dreams and goals* again.

Trust those early feelings that surfaced the instant you knew what to do with your life while you're in this world.

When you know what you came here to do and you start on that path, failure becomes a valuable lesson, not a setback.

You're going higher even if your feet are still on the ground. You're going higher because you're doing what your true core set out to do.

New Things Ahead

You've come too far, covered too much good ground, to avoid new things. Not only are you in position to receive new blessings - things you haven't thought about - you may also be nudged to try innovative things.

And you're ready! You're signed up to live a champion's life. Originality doesn't scare you. Even if you encounter hardships and setbacks, you find ways to navigate your way around these challenges.

Forging ahead is what you do. Of course, you won't be surprised to meet remarkable people, making lifelong friends. Offshoots of new dreams and goals surfacing in your mind won't send you into fear. You know you're an eternal being and you're ready to take on new, great experiences!

Dance in the light of dawn, new dreams rising like a bright sun, cloaking your life with hope.

Birth of the new calls up the spirit, your glorious energy, as you set sail toward new destinies.

Opening to newness awakens you to the splendor of the universe.

Look Around

You spend enough time searching for what you don't like, what you think is going wrong, don't you think? Isn't it time to notice blessings around you?

Focus on each career, creative arts product (i.e., album, book, knitted sweater, painting, homemade meal, play, movie, educational concept, health initiative and business service) you've created. Don't overlook anything. Refuse to make light of the blessings around you.

Good physical, mental and emotional health, financial strength, loving family and friends and an empowering hope are blessings. Actually think about the rewarding relationships you enjoy. Consider what you appreciate about your family and friends. Get specific.

Look around at the environments you move in. There's so much to appreciate.

Don't just smell the roses, see their brilliant color, celebrate their beauty. Touch their tender petals, soaking in their splendor – paying attention to the slightest detail you enjoy.

Appreciate the blessings that make up the fabric of life - coolness in a waterfall, a gentle awakening from the sun streaming through a window, a child's laughter – reading a poem.

Nothing is stronger than a heart that beats with appreciation.

Chapter 10 – Rewarding Relationships

Relationships are what life is about. There's never an instant when you aren't in a relationship. You're always relating to deeper parts of yourself. Even if you were abandoned as a child or left home as an adult, you're in relationship with your parents and siblings. Add in friends, neighbors, colleagues and passersby and the importance of developing rewarding relationships becomes clear.

Reflect on good relationships, even if they're relationships you admire other people for having. Spot behaviors and communication strategies that make relationships rich, strong.

Consider incorporating one or more of these behaviors and strategies into your relationships. Also try implementing ideas to improve relationships in your friendships and family connections. The payoff is huge.

Rich Connections

Person to person, organism to organism - relationships connect every living being. Mistreat yourself or another living being and it's akin to drilling a hole in the road, expecting the ride to be smooth. Look about you and see how everything alive connects, one to another.

Call a friend or relative, no matter their age, just to say "hello". Visit a neighbor. Ride to work with a colleague who lives nearby. Accept an invitation to dine with a pal or to explore paintings, sculptures and other local arts.

Who knows who you will meet while at these events, but first you have to accept the invitation. Remember this as you pursue your dreams and your goals – you can never have too many rich connections.

Relationships are the genesis of life.

"Who finds a faithful friend finds a treasure."

Jewish Proverb

Rich communications make life sweet, erasing misunderstanding – creating safe places to share ideas, dreams and daily happenings.

Love is displayed through more than a kiss. Sincere conversations, true care for another, joy that erupts in laughter put love on display. Oh, the wonder of rich connections!

"Others will measure you with the same rod you use to measure them."

Brazilian Proverb

Make Relationships Good

Good relationships, as highly desired as they are, do not just happen. Like flowers, trees and plants, relationships need nurturing to be good.

Make nurturing relationships a priority. This cannot be overstated. Many people have achieved great success by the world's standards only to end up feeling lonely, isolated and empty.

Achieving your goals will be especially sweet when you have people to celebrate and share your success with. Throughout life, relationships will link to the levels of joy that you experience. Make relationships good.

Apologize if you've spoken an unkind word or given a living being the type of care you wouldn't want to receive. Keep the air clear. Keep your relationships good, strong.

"What is now in the past was once in the future."

Indian Proverb

Love isn't realized until it's shared.

Though natural, relationships don't become good without you watering them with patience, understanding and love, sweet love.

Let Them Know

Let the people in your life know that you love them. Say "I love you!" to those you know. Show people how much you care.

Visiting, sharing a healthy meal, sending cards, personal notes and texts, telling loved ones how much they mean to you, are more ways to let people know that you love and care about them. Steer free of the trick of thinking that people magically "know" that you love them.

Make sure that people know what you think and feel about them. The power of this knowing could linger long after you have transitioned from this world.

It could fuel a loved one with hope, the strength to continue during the hardest times. The effects of you letting people know that you love them extends beyond you. It goes on and on.

Hidden love hurts. It's a heavy weight.

I love you and I want you to know.

"Where there is love there is no darkness."

Burundian Proverb

The greatest success is a loving relationship.

Chapter 11 – What's Next

Do you feel a sense of restlessness? Does it feel as if something new is stirring within you?

You may be eager to know what's happening. Believe it or not, you could be on the brink of a new awakening. Although what's coming next might not be clear to you yet, the unknowing around this birthing won't stop the launch - not if you stay open.

Stay open to goodness. Trust the Creator that you are loved and cared for – always.

Look to the present with a sense of great expectation. Finish the current phase that you are in, eagerly looking forward to what's going to happen next in your life.

Let The Next Vision Surface

Absent pushing, force or demand – let the next vision surface from within you. It's a vision that may have been there since before you entered this world. It's been waiting on you although you may not once have wanted it.

Until now . . .

You've crossed internal and external bridges, adjusted your sails, altered course without changing your destiny and you've mounted obstacles. Now, you're here, at a new place along your journey.

As an eternal being, you know there's more. What your consciousness may not know is specifically what's coming next. Be patient and trust. Let the next vision surface.

Within you is a lamp. It needs not rubbing. Trust instead. Soon you'll know what to do.

Trust sharpens inner vision.

Let the vision surface from within.

Physical sight is not equipped to lead you along the way.

Stay Open

Stay open now and while you sharpen your vision around your next goals. Disallow yourself to believe that your work here is finished.

Your one true Self can get through to you, directing your steps, if you stay open. The instant you convince yourself that you already know which way you should go, what you should do, you could close yourself off to hearing from Source.

Other gains related to staying open are a lighter heart, greater peace and more happiness. Time is going to pass. The world is going to fill up with events, rumors and a myriad of activities. You don't have to make anything happen.

Stay open so yours is a life filled with goodness, trust, light, love and the right actions – internal and external.

Communication channels from and to Source must be open to see how real they are.

A closed mind is an open door to sorrow.

An open mind is a limitless vault filled with wealth, a good life and blessings.

Your Work is Needed

Who told you that you're not a critical part of creation? Who told you that you're impotent, that your work isn't needed?

What you do *really* matters. There aren't words to fully express how important you and what you do are.

An older saying states, "Bloom where you are planted." That's right. Start where you are. After all, you're right smack dab where you are for a reason. Even if it's an uncomfortable place, your work is needed.

Continue to make joy and peace your aim. Seek love, joy, light and peace, making them your primary goals. Value and nurture relationships, including the one you have with yourself and Source. Thank you for the love-based good that you do! You're very important and always will be.

Life cannot be explained with words. Experience its splendor with each breath you take.

Without you there would be a hole in the universe.

You and what you do impacts everything else.

You Are Love – You Are Loved

One of the biggest deceptions is that you are a body. One of the biggest deceptions is that you aren't what you truly are. You are love; you are loved.

Errors in projection, nightmares, egoic influence – nothing – can change what Source created you as, created in Source's image, to be like Source. Be what you really are, shining in all its brilliance.

Be wonderful, natural you!

In this physical experience, delight in the path set before you. Remember that you are always loved. Let love's root bloom within you, blessing all you come in contact with.

If you don't hear the Creator saying "I love you" to you, be still. Listen.

Love is enough.

Feel the love the Creator has for you.

(Blank pages to create your personal mantras! These mantras elicit a powerhouse of emotion in you. They focus on a success area you want to gain strength in. Examples include a mantra to get started with power, a mantra to move through a challenge, a mantra to celebrate a recent success. Repeat these mantras as needed, fueling yourself with a bolt of motivation within seconds!)

_____

_____

_____

_____

_____

(Blank pages to create your personal mantras!)

(Blank pages to create your personal mantras!)

_____

_____

_____

_____

_____

_____

_____

(Blank pages to create your personal mantras!)

(Blank pages to jot down notes, ideas, goals and dreams)

_____

_____

_____

_____

_____

_____

_____

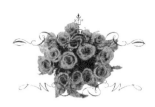

Read More Books- by Denise Turney

Love Pour Over Me

Portia (Denise's 1st book)

Long Walk Up

Pathways To Tremendous Success

Rosetta The Talent Show Queen

Rosetta's New Action Adventure

Design A Marvelous, Blessed Life

Spiral

Love Has Many Faces

Your Amazing Life

Awaken Blessings of Inner Love

Book Marketing That Drives Up Book Sales

Love As A Way Of Life

Escaping Toward Freedom

Whooten Forest Mystery: Ties That Bind

Heal Gorgeous: Wisdom Within You Knows the Way

Visit Denise Turney online – www.chistell.com

Made in United States
Orlando, FL
05 June 2025